关 于 鸟 的 短 诗

关 于 鸟 的 短 诗
Verses on Bird

ALSO BY ZHANG ER

Books in Chinese:

Seen, Unseen (QingHai Publishing House), 1999
Water Words (New World Poetry Press), 2002

Chapbooks in English translation:

Winter Garden (Goats and Compasses), 1997
Verses on Bird (Jensen/Daniels), 1999
The Autumn of GuYao (Spuyten Duyvil), 2000
Cross River . Pick Lotus (Belladonna Books), 2002
Carved Water (Tinfish), 2003

Verses on Bird

Selected poems by

张 耳

Zhang Er

Translated by
Rachel Levitsky
Timothy Liu
Leonard Schwartz
& Eleni Sikelianos
with the author

ZEPHYR PRESS
BROOKLINE, MA

Cover painting "Figure and Landscape"
          (1971) by Chuang Che
Book design by *typeslowly*
Text set in Adobe Caslon and SongTi
Printed by Cushing Malloy

Some poems in this book were previously published in a number
of American journals, including *The World* and *Van Gogh's Ear*, and
as chapbooks by the author. These poems were also published in the
Chinese original in numerous journals and newspapers, as well as
the two volumes of poetry in Chinese by the author. The translation
of "Verses on Bird" (with Sikelianos) was made possible, in part, with
public funds from the New York State Council on the Arts, a State
Agency. Thanks to The Transcendental Friend's Bestiary and the catalogue
for the exhibition on Contemporary Chinese Art and the Literary Culture
of China (Lehman College Art Gallery and Fisher Gallery of Bard College),
where parts of the translation of "Verses on Bird" first appeared.

Zephyr Press acknowledges with gratitude the financial support of Charles
Merrill, the Massachusetts Cultural Council, and the National Endowment
for the Arts.

NATIONAL
ENDOWMENT
FOR THE ARTS

massculturalcouncil.org

Library of Congress Control Number: 2004100899

08 07 06 05 04   98765432 first edition

ZEPHYR PRESS
50 Kenwood Street
Brookline, MA 02446
www.zephyrpress.org

Table of Contents

关 于 鸟 的 短 诗
from Verses on Bird
(1996-1997)

瞰　相

——题许以祺《拉萨天葬台》照

I.

鸟是以使命的严肃被呼喊来的
春天：一枚终于脱线的领扣，
手指从瘀血的桌腿剥出户外的力量：
光的事实不容拒绝，尽管视线焦点
在底片上加长了距离，使奔涌的颜色异化，
带给我们黑与白的定局感。

你想拥有一切，迅速按下快门。

超度的彩幡被镶进不透风的黑边，
天看起来不像天，像缺损的框架限定字眼
承受我们的感觉。或者暗中预备另外的规则
将词的位置彻底挤压出画面。

II.

我们每天都从取景器里看不见的山顶出发，
抢在太阳前向谷底冲去，狂舞想象的翅膀，
忽略以往每一次绑成知性的坠毁，
而鸟和鸟一闪就不见了，并非为了逃避
我们的惊慌。春天不过是一季的浑浊，
却经年累月捶击我们的头脑。

你想模仿鸟，你记不住这只鸟！

雨停顿在那个特殊海拔像一串删节号，
天空曾经充沛过词汇五彩的点滴。独处的鸟
比花冈岩体更果断地离开学会的仪式：
麻绳，麻布，铁棍，铁锤。

4

Bird's-eye View
for Xu Yiqi's photograph Lhasa Skyburial Platform

I.

Birds called in the spirit of a mission are
Spring: fingers unpeeling a collar button,
A gust from outdoors drawn from the legs of a desk.
Light, its fact, can't be denied, even if the focus
Extends the photo's negative distance, simplifying the riled colors,
Creating a sense of permanence in black and white.

You want to have it all, quickly snap the shutter.

Nirvana's streamers, set on the picture's black edge.
The sky does not look like sky but like a broken frame limiting words
As to foreground the senses. Or else secretly preparing other stratagems
To squeeze the position of the word out of the picture altogether.

II.

Unseen in the viewfinder we set off everyday from the mountaintop,
Race the sun to the bottom of the valley on imagination wings,
Overlooking every past crash of intelligence
While birds flicker, birds disappear, not trying to escape
Our flickering apprehension. Spring—the season
Of confusion—hammers the brain year after year.

You want to mimic the bird, you cannot remember the bird.

Like an ellipses rain halts at this particular elevation . . .
Empty sky that once brimmed with word's colorful drops.
Unlike the granite platform the solitary bird plays no part in the ritual,
Perches at an absolute distance:
Not in the Ropes, Rugs, Iron Sticks, Iron Hammers.

III.

想象在有树的低地支起帐篷，
再把它看成鸟。一旦跨进门槛躲开阳光直射，
我们就意识到这一切不过是没有形状的乏力感
对称于夜晚羊毛毯上酥油与酒意的混合，
缺乏下沉或者升华的份量。春的快乐时光
在巨石表面散发出积满雨的灰烬。

你不想死，你抓牢生活。

看鸟自天堂翻滚而下化成麻雀或鸡，
在增生的多数中寻觅独特的一行。
斜披袍襟也不能证明我们的确这样活过，
这样被获准在风景上坦露肩臂晒太阳。

IV.

现在你变成了鸟，有资格坐上山脊
看我怎样写岩石的柔软，丈量长短，
用一团没有刻度的生命。钢琴在某个地址上
固执地想把音乐敲打成交流的法器：
成功仿佛只取决于我能按准下一个黑或白的音键。

你寻求解脱，所以找到了降落的石台。

从戏剧性的阳光难以推测沉默外
鸟的声量。一场春雨冲刷去这里的墨迹
只剩下努力过度引导出的空洞。仰视，
言辞面对这个世界的无奈，将我与鸟隔开。

III.

Imagine building a tent in the valley with trees,
Then regard that tent as a bird. After crossing the threshold out
        of the direct sunshine,
We realized that all of this is no more than listlessness without shape
In symmetry with yoke butter, tipsiness on night's woolrugs,
Neither precipitate or distilled, weightless. Spring's joy
Evaporates from the boulder's platform like accumulated rain.

You don't want to die, you seize life.

Watching birds fall from the heavens and turn into sparrows or chickens,
Searching for a unique line within a multiplying mass.
A robe worn over one shoulder doesn't prove one is actually here
and is allowed to sunbathe on the beautiful rock.

IV.

Now you've become a bird and gained the right to sit on the mountain ridge
Waiting for me to write the tenderness of rock, measuring its dimensions
With an unquantifiable life. An insistent piano
Drums out the music as a mode of religious communication.
As if success solely depended on whether I could locate the black
        or white key.

You seek to extricate yourself, you find a descending rock platform.

In the striking sunlight, it is difficult to predict what sounds the bird
        will make outside
The staged silence. A single spring shower will wash away this trace of ink,
What will be left are the grooves eroded by the pen's overwork. Look up,
The helplessness of language when facing the world separates me
        from the bird.

(translated by Leonard Schwartz)

关于鸟的短诗

I.

看鸟的历程出入想象空间。秋意的阳光
希望，更暗示出云不断远离。
河水是绿的，像富含词汇的浓汤
排挤沿河树线的条理。如果这一切
真正属于词汇该多好 —— 一个元音
从背景改辙便唱尽一个世界的热闹。

没有鸟，因为鸟不上树，晾衣绳或烟筒。

那些结实的翅膀毛绒绒抖动
我们企图捉住的感觉。鸟存在，一闪，
依赖你能具体地看清自己，摸准下一个
欲念，追踪它升起，降落，不眨眼。

II.

观察者的主动性消亡为
由摄像机叠加出的飞行概念。
一条弧线展示鸟的物理和
这些紧随风势的串串定格。
一只眼透过镜片看另一只眼，看到的
竟比动词还要缺乏变化。

你错过鸟，鸟错过你。

或许应该取另外方向发现飞的秘密，
或研究很久以前羽管写下的静止：
笔锋行游，回旋，总在防备之外
将你推向一张白纸的无级落空。

Verses on Bird

I.

Bird-watching weaves in and out of imagined space. Autumn sunlight
Hopes, even hints, that clouds are detaching.
The river is green, a thick soup enriched with terminologies.
It squeezes out the orderly tree lines along the river. If only all these
Trees really belonged to the language—one vowel
Altering its sound track from the backdrop might sing out the surprise
              of all the world.

No bird, for the bird is not in the trees, on clotheslines, in chimneys.

Those solid feathered wings softly wave in
Events we are eager to net. Bird exists, a flicker,
If you can see through yourself, to follow the next
Desire, its rising, landing, do not blink.

II.

The observer's observation gives way to
The concept of flight accumulated (and reiterated) by the camera.
A curve exhibits the physics of the bird and
These freeze frames follow the wind's trends.
An eye watches another eye through the lens, what it saw
Varies less than the verb.

The bird misses you, you miss the bird.

Maybe one should look for another method by which to uncover
              the secret of flight
Or study the quietude written in quill long ago:
The stroke gliding and circling pushes you
Down an empty page, a stepless fall, into
Or out of the blue.

III.

所有旅行的照片都没留住鸟。记忆中的
鸣响谱进奏鸣曲便显得过分沉重，
无法复原切破的新鲜。而读诗时，
你并不关注内容，即使低音区里
如实凿打旅行故事缺乏戏剧性的情节，
日常家居的早晨或黄昏，出生或死去。

泪的成分与海水相似。

所以自然随意倒影在纸上一定歪斜成
不自然的表情。我们不得不刻意脱离
下面的石子路，草坪，花池子，放弃园艺
走上屋顶不去想时，忆起鸟飞过的一刻。

IV.

"河水流动。鸟肯定在飞。"
通过经典复格曲到达浪漫的努力
产生了舒伯特。风暴袭击时夜鹰尖叫
不断升级。这高贵的革命牺牲沉重，
却并不非要我在黑白键盘上
捕捉它的进程，而不移向另外的调性。

我找不出调性同一的鸟。

无知使我勇敢走向流水，没有预先理想
空缺过大，也不容另一次重复。此刻，
我的作为或不作，便掀起钢琴全部的波动
不被怀疑！鸟写诗，用一个元音。

III.

All the travel photos could not contain the bird. When wrought
Into a sonata its singing will seem heavy, it will
Not reveal the blush of a freshly cut wound. When reading poetry,
You do not pay attention to the story, even if the background hammers
Out the rhythm of a travelogue with no drama, the daily
Mornings at home, or at dusk, being born, or dying.

The mineral composition of tears is similar to that of the sea.

Therefore nature casually tumbled onto the paper must be twisted
Into unnatural positions. We'll have to deliberately detach the picture from
The cobblestone path, lawn, flower beds below, give up gardening,
Stroll up to the roof, not thinking, and then remembered the minute
The bird flew by.

IV.

The river is moving. The blackbird must be flying.
From classical fugues to Romanticism, this effort produced
Schubert. When storms attack, the nightjar's cry
Swells. The noble revolution will require great
Sacrifice, yet do not ask me to capture this process on the black
And white keys, nor to switch to another tone.

I could not find two birds with identical pitch.

With nothing to induce it, innocence makes me walk
Into rushing water as if I were brave. Empty space is great, but nothing
Repeats itself there. Whether I do
Or whether I don't; from each, the sum of the piano's voice will rise.
Not to be doubted: bird writes poem, one vowel at a time.

V.

天空中那种忽然的停顿，转向，
形状完整地载我进入无形的自由感。
"全部写出是一种方式。
留下不写是另一种方式。"
鸟　　　　地面盘旋　　　　光线
对称于　行与行　　　　　　　　　。

我触摸鸟的呼吸。

树叶不动地落下来，铺展词的翅膀
等待借口留驻我的窗台。暂时的窗，
暂时的停留。风吹过，水肯定在流。
两肩平伸的重心也会在焦盼中自在平衡？

VI.

安德烈·克得金由观察鸟走进书。
那是一种没有距离，揪住不放的天真。
这个活动的世界里，我们多么需要读者，
而这些埋头俯读的姿势却正为抵达
另外的国度祈祷，由于角度固定，看不清
脸面，风可能吹动书页，近似落叶。

让河休止在那一刻，这一刻。

因为以后的思想会打扰取景框里的亮度
比如雪将带来感光的新鲜。书脊平行线
相对我们慌张的一生有更合理的稳定，
因此鸟印在纸上，只暴露出鸟瞰。

V.

That sudden pause, in midair, turn,
A form puts me into a formless feeling—freedom.
"To put it all down would be one way
To leave it all out would be another, truer, way."
Bird   ground   circling   light
   something like   line by line

I touch the bird, which is breathing.

Leaves fall down without moving, spread the wings of the words
And await an excuse to pause on my windowsill. Temporary window;
Temporary pause. The wind blows; the water must be moving.
Can the weight between the stretched shoulders balance itself in this nervous
Anticipation?

VI.

First observing the bird, André Kertész then entered the book.
The reader has a simple fire, is consumed by words, words
Won't let go. In this world of motion, we keenly need readers; yet all these
        readers' heads
Bend over the book, praying to reach
Another world. Camera angle fixed, I can't make
Out the readers' features; a wind may flutter the book's pages, like leaves.

Let the river stop at that moment, at this.

Later on, a thought may skew brightness in the viewfinder, snow
Might bring new sensitivity to light. The parallel lines of the book's spine
Have more stability than our hurried lives—
Therefore a bird printed on the page exposes only
A bird's-eye view.

VII.

鸟紧贴河面的滑翔挑逗多种驱体感觉。
墨深如水，因而可以象征风暴在画框中
煽情："站在我身旁，你站在我身旁。"
词的分量被一只鸟和一腔歌唱的希望淹没
另外增加忧郁色块，像铁一样
沉下去，只舔湿简明主义的伤痕。

面对死，你怎么选择几片亮色羽毛？

而且能预料风暴之后发福的景致
在语言的泥滩上争食残余？词的歧意
移植入对自身动物性的理解，比如，
叉开双腿并非要求性交，或者充满爱情。

VIII.

脱光绿叶后，树才成为鸟的。
冷灰的天空能将所有耳朵塞满不听的毛
所有嘴喙聒噪你不想要的存在？
但鸟不是因为否认才被放在这样的高处：
那些古老的五花情趣向我们头顶洒下阴影
忽展忽拢，娇嫩得不能拿捏。

闭眼，一枪击毙一树的鸟。

由此躲避自身意义困挠是一种简明。
虽然分类学细目出发于省减意愿，
逼近的冬天对岩鸽与蓝雀的鉴别
却不一定使我们归属删除枝叶的实质。

VII.

A bird glides along a river's surface, from which it knows a dozen bodily things.
Ink dark as water, therefore, may symbolize that the storm in the picture frame
Flirts, singing "Stand by me."
The weight of the word was submerged by the bird and a (full cavity of)
      desire to sing
Now add some melancholish colors on this side; like iron
They sink, and we barely lick the minimalism's new scar.

Facing death, how would you chose a few bright feathers?

And be able to foresee sitting fat and pretty after the storm
Fighting for the last crumbs in the mud of language? A word's double means
Plant the consciousness of our animal nature; spreading
One's legs might or might not be "Give me sex," or, for love.

VIII.

Stripped of leaves, only then does the tree belong to the bird.
Can the lead-gray sky stuff all ears with feathers not to hear
Each beak clamor an existence you do not solicit?
Bird is elevated to this height (the tree, symbols) but not in order to not covet:
Ancient temperaments, tradition, shower shadows on us:
Sudden spread, sudden retreat, a shadow's too fragile to pick up.

Eyes shut, one shot destroys a tree full of birds.

Thus one escapes troubling over the meaning of a self in the leanest of acts.
Even though itemized taxonomy originated in an eagerness to simplify
Winter approaching, defining robin, pigeon
Will probably fail to file us back at the root, rid of branches and leaves.

IX.

看不见海的时候，水才从四面包围了我。
不必在水淹中挣扎或怀抱责任感，
生命，一句太短的漂流，
有光承托翅膀的重量，是什么
保证梦的两翼按他们的水平扭曲？
同时将语言野生的根在流浪间潜没？

月光折射入水时，我听见了天籁，

像呼吸赤裸到无字。皮肤暖上来
只挤紧双股，生怕错过机运。
而鸟飞起把留下的放任引向纸面。
从梦的海上鸟飞起，淋漓着血性欲河！

X.

花草与茶杯拼贴一幅时间差异：
草剪还是不剪？夏天的难题
不需鸟问讯，因为很少鸟鸣。
换羽毛的夏天，雨水冲洗鸟的空间。
实用的鸟，尽快长大
占据最多虫和果实的夏天。

你回忆鸟独立树梢夸耀性器的初春。

夏在日记里抄录野花的名称
动人得没有理由，即使现在
模样已被忘掉，夏天来不及思想的采集
让我们冬日里烹茶相对，并企图说些什么。

IX.

When the sea is out of view, water surrounds me on all sides.
No need to struggle for breath, or hold onto a sense of responsibility;
Life, a short sentence, drifting;
There is light to stand the weight of the wing; what would
Guarantee that the dream flies according to the wing's water-level twist,
Or sink language's wild roots in itinerant waves?

When the moonlight was mirrored on the water's surface, I heard the sound
          of nature,

A wordless breathing, naked. Skin warms
Up only to squeeze the thighs tight, a lost opportunity,
While the bird takes off, leaving all the indulgence to the page.
From the dream of the sea, the bird traveled, dripping desire like a river; blood.

X.

Flowers, grasses, and tea cups are collaged from summer into a winter's frame.
Should the grass be cut? Summer's dilemma.
Not a concern for the bird, for there are few birds singing.
Summer of changing feather, rain washes bird space.
Practical bird, grows up in a hurry.
Bird possesses summer, summer possesses fruit and insects.

You remember early spring when the bird stood on a branch to advertise its sex.

Names of wild flowers noted down in a summer diary
Are suddenly moving, even now in winter;
Their set has been forgotten, the summer's collection never re-thought
But they make us sit down with tea in deep winter, facing each other;
          we even try to say
Something.

XI.

伴鸟鸣醒进一个不适合出门的日子，
才意识到到我们终将一天天老去。
床的自身状况迫使躯体失落家园，
一天天生存的阴雨有如钝痛不退的牙齿；
生活在顶屋的日子——晨起窗台都天蓝，
黄昏的尾翼贴紧季节不变的心情。

得相隔某种距离才能认清眼前的事物。

而由卧室抵达澡间持续升级的程序一定
牵扯起内脏沿着走廊复杂的对映。
我匀称蠕动，由衷地没有距离——
这一天天地生存，一天天地老去。

XII.

画家索菲娅从自画的泉眼痛饮，水光吹开，
阳光允诺地淌下一条金河，华盛顿广场
顿时显出迁徙之后的春情。
头顶上空白仍就空白，弯下腰
是因为需将尘土的褐黄成分混入油彩，
晃一晃，一笔竟拖出那么多不确定的线条。

你何时到达？你要飞往某种海蓝的意象？

一次切实的努力和自由地擦去重绘
或许能确保调色板虚实适度
在闭合的位置上放生空白（喷泉或鸟），
而不仅仅红红绿绿地应答模印技术？

XI.

Wake up, bird's singing, to a day not fit for outdoors.
We will all grow more or less languidly old.
The bed kicks the body out,
The drizzle of day to day, a slow, infinite toothache;
Penthouse days—each a.m. is sky-blue on the windowsill;
The bright orange tail of dusk presses close to a seasonless mood.

One has to keep a certain distance to recognize things within a field of vision.

Yet the elaborate procedure of getting from bed to bathroom must stretch
Along a hallway which reflects inner organs.
I peristalize, wholeheartedly, no distance from the body—
Live day to day, day to day, get old.

XII.

Painter Sophia drinks from the mouth of the spring she painted herself,
        spray and light spread,
The generous sun pours down a promise, golden river, Washington
Square immediately exhibits spring after a long migration.
Empty is still empty overhead. Bend
To mix the earth-brown into the oil base,
From back to forward, backward to forth, one stroke pulls out so many
        uncertain lines.

When are you going to arrive? Are you flying toward a sea-blue image?

A real effort and the ease of erasing and repainting
Can not only fulfill the colorful monotype technique
But can perhaps ensure the appropriate balance of solid vs. void on the palette
And in the enclosed space free the void (fountain or bird).

XIII.

早在我们心目中丧失尺度，缺乏升空纯情，
扭曲，衰竭，出生笼禁，未曾学会张开
翅膀，习惯久坐翻弄羽毛和肚脐，
争红斗绿有时只为口粮，又不忘及时出让，
印作招贴画，塑了金身，灌入唱片
电动升上旗杆，演义成神或魔⋯⋯

与飞无关，与歌唱无关，与梦无关⋯⋯

被我们从天上网捕，击中要害，挖空内容，
涂各式调味汁，再烹入我们的算计，
被我们嫉妒又世代仰视，因而心怀暧昧，
具体或抽象地不懂得节制！

XIV.

看他们一齐飞起，蓝雀，岩鸽，乌鸦⋯⋯
破落的梧桐上空，停滞继承了种族间隔的
公众话语。日落，长出多元阴影
才显现这个系统地平线的彩色。
我们坐着，挣扎在外，计划下一步表达，
虚拟脚趾向柏油路的切点。

该讲的他们都流动地讲过了。

只有空巢以某种浮浮沉沉的角度在树枝上
让我们彻夜讶异：那藏起来的或许能
把他们的姿式不褪色地剪接给我们？
长长短短，脚趾紧抓，像他们那样争论着落实？

20

XIII.

Dropped from the heights in our esteem, lust for soaring run out
Tangled, exhausted, cage-born, never learned to spread
A wing, habituated to sitting and tinkering with its own feathers
Feathers flying over food supplies, feathers for sale,
Printed on posters, sculpted in gold, cut into disks,
Electrically raised on the flagpoles, evolved into divinity and devil . . .

Will have nothing to do with flying, not with singing, not dreaming . . .

Snatched from the sky in nets, whacked at the life spot, dug of all contents,
Smeared with rich sauces, cooked into calculations,
Envied and respected for generations, filled with dubious wishes
Concretely or abstractly, birds do not understand the value of control!

XIV.

From the tired-out oak, they take off simultaneously: blue jays, rock pigeons,
            crows . . . their inter-
Species chatter hangs mid-air and abuses the public language which has inherited
Our races. Out of the sun which sets grow multi-shade shadows
Illustrating the horizon's colors in this system.
We sit, we struggle, and plan the next expression,
Toes fictively make contact points on the paved road.

All that ought to be said, they've said it already, flowingly.

But the empty nest, its angle specific to the branch, bobbing up and down
Makes us wonder all night: maybe what is hidden can
Still throw a posture, a shadow projected directly onto us—
Talons tightening, like blue jay, rock pigeon, to settle down on solid ground, arguing

XV.

吸引我们下腹肿胀，爆破力在内部
像滑雪板溜向冰封的黑森林
树齐刷刷往后退却。这是我们模式的缺失：
陷入自身重力，经不起捻摩的白色鹅毛
腾起像泡沫，倾刻化为不纯的汁。
泪溅到脸上，在有意无意之间。

双黑钻石，黑得不再会闪耀的双重三角。

今晚没有什么新计划，今晚以后也没有，
我们已经翻过各自的山顶，看过那片彩霞，
现在能做的是下山。寻找一条更惊险的路。
沉默中，雪紧追雪的贴切使我无法直视你。

XVI.

这些探向沼泽的平行线条从一开始
就注定驶向自己的对立：变幻歌唱的方式
也难界定人声与鸟声，像换一个播段会导致
主体客体的转换。我们接近飞机场时，
尘雾中果然展现一幅接近完整的图画：
TWA, American Air, 白鹭鸶, 高压电网。

即使跳出皮肤，手也只把握老迈的五行。

这些线条的平行不是为了追逐鸟，
不过是形式的旅行，从日到夜，冬到春，
五行分出八行，十四行，河流成海的运动。
封闭干线上速度的变形丧失了鸟对于我们的真实性。

XV.

Gravity swells the lower gut, an explosive interior force
Slides down toward the ice-covered forest; black;
Trees whistle by. This is the flaw in our model:
Sunk into the weight of the self, the downy snow could not handle twists
        and turns;
Flying up in foam, it instantly relents into an impure liquid.
Slashes on the face, unintentional / intentional.

Double black diamonds, double triangles, some things are too black to shine.

Tonight there is no plan. After tonight there is no plan either.
We've climbed over each of those hills, where the evening glows.
Now we descend; Is there a more adventurous route?
In silence, snowflake chases snowflake, I cannot look at you.

XVI.

Stretching from the beginning toward the marsh, these parallel lines
Are doomed to drive to their opposites: switching the singing to show
Boundary between voices, human or bird, will be difficult, since changing
        the channel leads to an exchange
Of subject and object. We approach the airport in the smog; as anticipated, a
Nearly perfect picture:
TWA, American Air, electrified wire network, white egrets.

Even if you jump out of your skin, the hand can only grasp five ancient lines.

These parallel lines are not to indicate chasing after the bird.
They are merely the translocation of forms: day to night, winter to spring.
Five lines become eight, fourteen, the movement of a river rushing to sea.
Speed on the turnpike deforms shapes, abolishes the authenticity of the bird.

XVII.

向前，以一种固定的姿态等候，
因为等候才有鸟飞来。窗玻璃外
闪耀着草坪上家庭野餐的浪漫情结……
帕斯克尔说，"我们不能获得财富，也不能
获得真理，"那么、就用喉咙的九个音调肯准
这些桌面上的消遣吧！这一刻。在这里。

悲观的理性主义从反面为天空穿起鸟的衣裳。

琐碎是另外的美学问题，不加思索地写出，
比如辞典里边剪刀和花花绿绿的羽毛。
所以那些关于死亡的警号过分仓促，
仿佛全体的鸟只突现鹰钩嘴喙的布局。

XVIII.

雷响起，紧跟着天幕上驰骋的亮鸟，
就这样宣布：鸟－死－了。
这时候，河的确在我眼前消失为幽绿的前景
陪衬树上那只红胸脯的知更鸟从早唱到晚。
街顿时湿得像河，带着婉转的拖腔。
背书包的白裙女孩水洗一样漂过。

这涉及水性的光影变幻。

书桌的阴暗不朴素地反射前景的阴暗。
词打落在词上，像窗玻璃外为鸟杜撰葬仪的点滴。
我们可有可无，而鸟听上去像阵雨涤除暑热，
或者是死伸展翅膀在雨中抖去铺陈。

XVII.

Lean forward, strike a pose, wait.
Because of waiting, a bird arrives. A romantic mood
Twinkles on the lawn of the family picnic outside this window . . .
Pascal said, "We cannot obtain wealth, nor
Can we obtain truth"; then let us employ the nine tonality
        of the throat to affirm
These entertainments of the table. This moment. Here.

Pessimistic idealism clothes heaven from an opposite end.

Triviality is another aesthetic matter, scribbling without thinking,
Like the bright feathers and scissors (birds and scraps) in dictionaries.
All those warnings about death seem hurried,
As if from the body of the bird protrudes only a sketch of the hawk-like beak.

XVIII.

Thunder, following the galloping silver bird across heaven's canopy,
Thus declares: BIRD-IS-DEAD.
For the moment the river does disappear from my window into a dark green
Foreground. In contrast: the red-breasted robin singing on the tree
        from dawn till dusk.
The street suddenly as wet as the river, trailing sweet riffs.
The girl in a white dress with a bookbag drifts by as if washed there.

This may involve the shift of watery light or shadow.

The gloomy desk reflects a distortion, a gloomy future.
Word upon word, the droplets outside the pane make a funerary
        arrangement for the bird.
(It doesn't matter) If we exist, if we don't, the bird sounds like rain rushing
        away the summer's heat
Or death spreads its wing in the water to wash away the elaborating dust.

XIX.

总是先有急急躁躁的电闪雷鸣，
才落下这些从容的点滴，把合唱队的唱和
揉入不干的海面。啊，提高你的声量，
自然的管风琴！有这么些天才，这么些爱
禁不住淌下来，死就让它去死 ——
交响乐尾声的高潮迫使我流出内心。

拱门下，我出让六弦琴和湿漉漉的嗓音。

小心地潇潇或在有雨的下午挑拣词句。
然而透过你有秩序的冰凉又细碎，
我还是看见了那无帆的桅杆直立地漂下河口
所以我等待退潮后你月光般在海面无声张扬。

XX.

到哪里寻找足够的字眼去命名眼前种种事物
或者足够的词汇去形容另外一些词汇？
甚至在急雨打落牡丹最后一点粉红后，
还有这样细长淡藕合下垂钟形不知道是什么的
串集被宽厚带条理浓绿的层次托起，
柱头残片，裂缝的水泥地，吊在半空的破球网。

你说，"无语时，一只天使正飞过。"

无论是阴是晴。只要把耳朵里音量开大，
呆板的天空就呼呼地响起风声，
聚焦无限远，进而借助这条风景线往下看，
"是的，我们曾经访问过那个村落，
　　　贴河，朝海，蒙着雨。"

（一九九七年七月二十五日定稿于曼哈顿华盛顿高地城堡屯）

XIX.

First, the impatient lightnings and thunders.
Then the drops come leisurely down, the harmony of the chorus kneading
Into the never-dry sea. Ah, lift up your voices,
Organs of nature! So much talent, so much
Love indefatigably drips; let it die down—
The symphony's final tide forces me out.

Under the arch, I offer lute and the moist voice.

Drizzling, or choosing words carefully in the rainy afternoon,
Yet through your orderly cool and fine details
I can see the sailless mast, erect and sliding down toward the river's mouth.
So I wait, wait for your silent display on the moonlit sea after the tide has drifted.

XX.

Where can we find enough names to name all these things in front of our eyes?
Or enough adjectives to modify all these adjectives?
Even after the shower has stripped the last bit of pink off the peonies
There are still these unknown long and tiny pale violet downward curving
        bell-shaped clusters
Held up by those wide and humble striped sheaves,
Remnants of a pillar cup, cracked cement, collapsed basketball net
        hanging mid-air.

You say, "When we are silent, an angel is flying by."

Whether rainy or clear. Turn up the volume in the ear,
The dull sky will resound with gusting wind.
Focus interminably far, with the help of the horizon line, look down,
"Yes, we visited that village,
                adjacent the river, facing the sea, in a fine drizzle."

(translated by Eleni Sikelianos)

27

from Riverglyph / Water Words
(2001)

施工中的江桥

接通了就取消了悬念
现在彩旗飘飘，向没有限制的
河心探试。要接到对岸吗？
还是就如此舒坦本色的双肩
让船从下面滑过，看不见
水花。鸟在上面
自然而然。山不动，拥着
不断更新的住宅楼房。

是这样吗？我的爱？
平静的表层，黄水、黄土
第七层五千年
第十层八千年
沉积翻起来
发现美，小陶壶、鱼尾。
我投入你的怀抱
靠住钢筋铁臂痛哭一场——
因为你腰围
流水一样的情

深不见底的第九十九层。

A Bridge Under Construction

When the two ends join, the suspense will be eliminated
where colorful flags flutter above the boundless
heart of the river. Will it reach the other shore
or just spread its broad shoulders
and let the boats glide under without any visible
wake? Birds are above
naturally. Mountains do not move but embrace
the residential flats constantly being redone.

Is that it, my love?
Calm surface, yellow water, yellow soil:
the seventh layer   five thousand years
the tenth layer   eight thousand years
as the sediment churns up
rediscovered beauty: a ceramic pot, a fish tail.
I throw myself into your arms
and lean against your chest of steel weeping
for your girth traverses
tenderness like the flowing waters—

the bottomless depth of the ninety-ninth layer.

五金杂货

五脏六腑你向我摊出一切 ——
锁和各种式样的把手，落满尘土
早已推不开那扇门。这里的陈列
不代表时间的积累，或者
为某种将来的功用，不过支撑
垮下来的自重，干瘪的眼屎，百年
祖屋，虫蛀剩下的感情。
展示一切是为了不给出 ——
因为尘土、自重、眼泪和旧爱。
这景象一现，为了必定消失 ——
大水将至，蓝色的水位线
画在屋顶：一丝嘲弄，一丝
嘻笑，一对展不开的愁眉。
大水将至。所有的沉积都要
被江水洗净，炸掉，用TNT
然后
再次成为沉积
为什么不？
八十岁的父亲，六十岁的儿子
肩并肩指给我看孙子建筑的
新城－江南春绿，水泥墙，玻璃窗
取代此岸陈旧的木头、虫蛀以及
对往日抽象的温情。
顺流船啊
顺流船
你看我没有退一步的
坚持，眯起眼，用螺丝刀
齿轮，钟表零件的精细
揪心掏肝的冷静。

The Hardware Store

You spread your guts out for me, everything—
knobs and handles covered with dust
unable to open any door for years. Displays
don't present the accumulations of time
or any future function, only sustain
the self-weight crushing down, dried-up sleepy buds, those
hundred-year-old ancestor homes moth-infested,
showing all has been given up
to dust, respect, tears and old love.
Such evanescent displays must vanish
for the flood is coming, blue water marks
painted above the roof: a mockery,
a grin, a pair of eyebrows forever knotted.
The flood is coming. All the accumulated sediment will be
washed clean, dynamited with TNT
then
becoming deposit again.
Why not?
An eighty-year-old grandpa, a sixty-year-old son
standing there shoulder to shoulder, pointing out to me
a new city built by the grandson
high-up on the south shore, spring green, cement walls, glass windows
replacing the wood now rotting on this shore, moth-eaten
and nostalgic
for the downstream boat.
Oh, downstream boat,
you look at me, never stepping back,
insisting, narrowing your eyes like a screwdriver
or a tooth-ripped saw, the delicate interior of a watch
composed as a calmness churns in my guts.

滑 坡

早就听说过，像别人的故事：
先起烟，黄土蓬飞，在浓绿间
从想不到的位置倒下来。我们
滑行，顺流向前。屏住呼吸听见
石头、土方、心，滚落
砸进摸不清的
浊水。
浪
溅
高度无法丈量。
曝光，胶片噌噌变色，像蛇
不容你多想，记录下来
一生都在等这一刻。谁诱惑谁？
水引导你向下，来到这里，
却不告诉你这一切为
什么，又象征什么。也许
它能诠解你一生中
最大的错误 —— 简直像个
初出茅庐的业余爱好者
所有的经验和训练
滑坡：
没入不容多想的
旋涡。哪里是
你早以为练就的控制？
砸进去，砸进来
河身
疾水、深水
冲撞。
屏住呼吸
看滑坡：
黄土绿树，既定的位置
已成为别人的故事。

Landslide

Heard it all before, someone else's story:
first there's dust, yellow soil flying in the thick green,
crashing down from an unexpected place
as we slide downstream and forward, holding our breath to hear
stone, soil, and our hearts pounding down,
unable to grasp
turbid water,
waves
splashing
height immeasurable.
Exposed, the film changes color, like the snake
that won't allow you to think, record
what you have waited for all your life. Who seduces who?
The water induces you to come down to this place
yet doesn't tell you why
or what all this symbolizes. Maybe
it can explain your whole life's
biggest mistake—simply like
an amateur newly-minted,
your past experience and training
landsliding
into a whirlpool
that does not allow for thinking. Where now
is all of your well-cultivated control?
Smashing in, splashing out
into the river body's
rapid water, deep water
crashing down.
Holding your breath
as we watch:
yellow soil, green trees, the established order
already becoming someone else's story.

云 昌 号

一夜之后，还停在码头
没出发的绿漆铁顶
已将船客送去
又接回，自不能抵达的地方
回来。光从高处透出向往。窗外
江水、江航，码头上挑夫
一步走出你和我的距离。一步。
投身进去，醒在爱人身旁
白象一样的山，愈看愈远
愈看愈不像。怎么能认出你呢？
我的情欲，藏在没出发的
铁顶下，水的核心，青枝绿叶
掩映响亮的热情。

On Board the Yun Chang (Lush Cloud)

After the night, it remains docked,
steel roof painted green. Fails to depart
yet sends the guests back
and forth, back from an unreachable
place. Light illuminates the yearning from on high. Outside the porthole:
lush clouds, riverboats, porters on dock
stepping into the distance between you and me. One step.
Throw oneself in. Or awaken next to a lover,
a mountain like a white elephant moving away as you watch
the resemblance disappear as you watch. How can I recognize you?
My desire hidden underneath a steel roof
that never departs, the nuclear of the water, green branches and jade leaves
screening out the loud passion.

西 瓜 汁

你说，从没见过这样吃西瓜
捧着喝，汗从鼻尖、额头、后背
滚下来。读过 Frida Kahlo 吗？看过
她的西瓜，大张嘴、厚唇、黑色的籽
很多，因为她孤独。
你用利刀把瓜切成整齐的块
吃得很斯文。
我啃，像狗，Kahlo 的瓜
然后喝
捧起来喝。
瓜不太新鲜
对，多年前就打开了 -
那么，把瓜磨碎，榨汁
倒进象形的锥状玻璃杯
红汁、吸管，也很斯文。
这时，我们听到鸟
听到更远的山崩
在脚下轰响。又炸了，住房或
旧工厂。某些活过的部分
比如西瓜。
你像个饿坏的孩子，还说不饿。
饿？你不可能懂，饿。
深深舔了又舔愈涌愈多的汁液，饿。
但这不妨碍我们的切口
正当，长久。甚至美丽。
不信？
潮涌上脚面……
It's going to be difficult
又怎么样？容易的都已做过
容易地完成，又轻易地放下。
它们在哪儿？不留情丢下的
西瓜皮？
慢慢吸
一小口
又一小口

Watermelon Juice

You say you've never seen watermelon being eaten this way:
held up to the face, drunk with sweat pouring down nose tip, forehead
and back. Have you read Frida Kahlo? Seen her watermelon
wide open, full-lipped, black seeds
so manifold for she was lonely.
You cut it up with a sharp knife into neat cubes,
so genteel. I gnaw mine
like a dog, that melon of Kahlo's,
then drink it up.
Not even fresh.
True, this morning isn't even opened.
Let's then grind it, squeeze out the juice
and pour it into an inverted cone glass:
red fluid, thin straw, and so genteel.
Now we can hear the birds above
and the landslide in the far
roaring under our feet. A residence dynamited again
or an old factory. Some parts survive:
a watermelon, for example.
You're like a starving kid, but still you say that you're not hungry?
Hungry? Can't possibly understand that: hunger.
Lick deeply into the oozing juice again and again, hungry.
It won't keep our cuts from being normal and correct.
Nor beautiful.
No?
The tide rushing up to our feet . . .
It's going to be hard.
So what? Easy things have been done already,
easily finished and easily dropped.
Where are they now? The melon rind
carelessly thrown away?

越吮越浓，越短的底线
越精致的锐角，甜的边沿。
没有什么要求，意思是说
要求全部。楼上的全部。
楼下。
这是药
喝下去，喝下去治愈
所有的伤。现在你挣扎
一边享受，一边怕心身的依赖。
这可以理解：
喝江水长大的，都拼命往
沙漠移民。太挤，太多解不开的
缆绳和在疾水中失控的不确定。
沙漠，地下暗河，都流过，水
还有果汁。
沙漠。
那时候，
你还会捧起她的脚，认出她？
藤萝架，上海浦
忍红潮涨起直入身体。

Slowly sucking
one small portion
after another,
it's getting thicker, the edges
sweeter. Asking for nothing
means asking for all, all in the upstairs.
Downstairs.
This is the medicine—
drink it, drink it down for it will heal
all wounds. Joy now struggling
alongside the fear of being attached
which is understandable:
whoever grew up drinking from the river
must migrate to the desert. Too crowded, too many knots
that can't be untied, the uncertainty
of losing control in its rushing current.
Desert that an underground river
passes through, water
juice too.
Desert.
And then
will you hold her feet up again and recognize her?
Wisteria arch, Shanghai port
bearing the red tide as it swells
into the body.

(translated by Timothy Liu)

涉江 · 采芙蓉

I

即使这个不常来的花园，也踩出
一条惯常的路。就这么可叹。

就是从专心弈棋的神仙桌旁
不进入地走过，把思想按下去

就像把计时钟按下去。喷泉在晨光中
休止：淤泥、昨夜的落叶和垃圾。

表演者还没出现，看客和小偷的
情节在想象中展开。一秒钟。

路边的货摊刚刚摆出还没化妆的脸：
这串彩石该配哪件衣服？

山水、花鸟、许多容易的喜爱
是不是也是你的喜爱？她不确定

进而更换审视之后的答案。仅仅
花费时间，那是谁都有的－

喷泉女神风化发黑的瘦脸
头上的绿葡萄已在三个月里

变成红宝石。供你选择的
已经有限，包括被你否定的一瓣。

另一瓣悬在颈下，依然在胸前不忘
采或不采的辛苦，其中的清香。

Cross River . Pick Lotus

That even in this unfrequented garden, a single path is
Beaten down by habit. Is pitiful.

As is walking by this table where divinities concentrate
On a game of chess, pressing down on thinking

As if pressing on a timer. The fountain sleeping in this morning's light:
Last night's leaves, sludge, garbage.

The performer doesn't show; imagination hatches a plot—
Spectator, thief. A second.

Sidewalk vendor begins to display the naked head:
What matches the chain of colored stones?

Mountains and Rivers, Flowers and Birds, delights various as they are easy.
Are you delighted? She doesn't know.

Further examination changes the mind.
It only takes time, the least we have.

Slender face of fountain goddess erodes and
Darkens. Her grape locks turn from green to red

In just three months. Your selection already limited,
Includes the lotus petal refused

Another is suspended below the neck, memory on your chest
Hard decision whether to pick, slight fragrance in choice.

2

那些跑步经过的锻练者
脸上一般表情充足甚至幸福

身材各式各样，并不仿照我们
心目中完美的向往。

写诗是不是也与晨跑一样？
笨拙而不优雅地吭吭吃吃

在经过的路上留下旁人不解
更缺乏自我审视的一行又一行。

为了总在前面的目的:
每一天到来，又一次锻练。

她风风火火地走，夹一卷逾迦功
天蓝里透出抑制的反叛

从头传到脚，向太阳
五体投地也需要柔软的腰肢和

结实的欲望。而你面壁十年
在穿衣镜前还是凸腹凸臀屈膝

四面甲壳的防卫，优雅与你
整年的工作无关。

与你今天出门无关。

2

Joggers pass. Generally content
In the face, even happy

Various in body, not the image of the ideal sought
In the heart of our mind.

Is writing poetry like jogging in the morning?
Clumsy. Ungracefully huffing and puffing

Embark along a road without glancing back
Cross line after incomprehensible line—before onlookers.

Reaching into the constant goal ahead
Arrival of another day, another exercise.

She walks by quickly, clutching a yoga roll
That is sky blue, the rebellion suppressed

Top to bottom, prostrate to the sun
Needing elastic waist and

Solid desire. Facing the wall for eons fashioning
Belly and buttocks protruding, knees bent before the mirror

Defended by shells on four sides. From grace estranged
This entire year's work

And your outing today.

3

坐下来点心。在葡萄藤的院子里
等待阳光把你暖和起来。

看盘盘盏盏的碎菜，水果，炸土豆
摊鸡蛋，果汁，咖啡，蛋糕

看见兰泽，芳草，深林，云霏霏
奥林比亚的上帝们吵吵闹闹

完好端上来，狼藉撤下去。
我们竟有这么多必需？

善于把美变成丑陋。然后去
卫生间做另外一些事情。

我和他们无一例外地喝茶
吃饼，再叫一份咖啡。

然后问，这架葡萄是真的？
这顿早餐代价多少？

滴着血，刚从他胸膛里摘来。
要尝尝吗？我的神，滴着血

要去哪里？小心醉倒
低着头。

3

Sit and eat something in the vineyard.
Wait for the sun to warm you.

Watching the dishes and bowls, cut fruit,
Vegetables, fried potatoes, eggs, juice, coffee and cake

Orchid patches, fragrant grasses, dense forest
Clouds, sleet—the Olympians quarrelling

Laid out in perfection, removed by messy defeat.
Wondering whether all of it is necessary?

Capable as we are of turning beauty ugly,
Going to the toilet to do another thing.

Like them, I drink tea, unexceptionally—
Eat cake, then order another coffee.

And ask if the overhead vines are real and
How much for the breakfast?

Bloody, having just been plucked from his chest.
Want a taste? My god, bloody

Where are you going? Drunk and head lowered
Be careful. Don't fall.

4

脱下华美的衣冠，便下起一场小雨。

窗台上吊兰淋着耀眼的阳光。
真的暖和起来了，你说。

并不特别针对怀里的情侣。不过
自我陶醉，开满野花的草地

漂向江流。摘吧，尽兴奉献
桃李之后的盛夏，不是野花的荷莲。

静坐。一种姿势就是
千种姿势的象征。

你对我说，等。所有答案
就是等，盘腿——

花露把床单印出一滴滴流水的
原则。拈花一笑

你睡进我此刻的梦，在极乐的
意义上，抓紧我的手。

蝴蝶一样忽乎将至、忽乎将行
献出哪怕仅仅一季的柔情。

就是工作。罗丹说永远工作
就是欲望永不满足。

与之呼应，雨起伏着
岁月流逝的忧愁

4

Taking off a splendid costume while rain drizzles down.

Ferns on the windowsill dripping with sun—
You say, 'It's really warmed up now,'

Not particularly to the lover in your arms.   A mere
Indulgence, on the meadow sparkly with flowers

Drifting down the river. Pick, pick to your heart's content
This offer of mid-summer after peach and plum, a domesticated lotus

Sits still. In one position
That symbolizes thousands.

You tell me to wait. Answers lie
In waiting. Cross the legs like this—

Drop by drop, dew on flowers imprints the idea of water
Flowing onto sheets. Pick up lotus, smile

With a sense of Sukhavati, you fall into my momentary
Dream, grasp my hands.

The butterfly that suddenly arrives, suddenly departs
Offering a tender love for only a brief season.

That is the work. Rodin said *toujours travailler*
Desire never satisfied.

Undulating rain which echoes it, rises, falls
Alongside the sadness of time passing

Sacrificial, yet dignified, throws itself down the river.

5

满月。周末的家庭组合。
把孩子放在哪？

月亮东升，也还没有结论。
老实的想法只做为枕头

供你辗转，进而写下些
老实的句子。今晚

只读吕德安和里尔克。因此也想到
神、绝对理念以及现成的秩序。

I am not looking because I am married.

不看的世界在月光下栩栩如生：
总是忧伤以终老 ——

同居而离心抑或同心离居
峻山，霰雪，幽林，芳草

会有这一片动人的水衬在下面
把今夜托起，你和你和云豹。

那么，孩子放在哪？

除了抱在怀里
在我身体气味里上上下下？

5

Full moon. The composition of a happy family on a weekend.
Where to put the child?

In the east, the moon rises without solution.
Honest thoughts become mere pillows

For tossing and turning, before writing down
A few honest sentences. Tonight

Reading only Lu De-an and Rilke. Therefore thinking
About god, absolute ideals and the present order of things.

结了婚，就不找了

The unseen world vibrant under moonlight:
Endings are always sad.

Bodies together and hearts apart or vice versa
Snow, mountain peak, a deep forest, lavender and lemon grass

That the cradle of moving waters underneath—would eternally
Hold the night, you and you and the cloud leopard

Where then, to put the child?

Besides close to my chest
Up and down wrapped in my smell.

6

还是想象他涉江采芙蓉吧
路滑，明月忽乎消失，湘夫人

卷入乌云，又怎么能怪我？
一半零落，一半骋望

也不管赠谁，你和你和她
想或着不想，这是不是生活？

他一定也唱着，让江风
野外的气息吹拂两腿间的花果

水光。到底都是爱。美人。一个人走
还是集体殉节，都是爱。

都在心里唱了，从挂满葡萄的园子走出
出于同样的原因。一场大火。

一个好天，夏末的一个夜晚
看世界和悲哀向你靠拢

在最后一块完整的石头上
凝立，趁月正高

留下光辉的自我，拈花一笑
可人的面庞，奇服，巍冠，夜明珠

天花乱坠，乱坠。

6

It's better to imagine him crossing the river to pick lotus.
Slippery scene: the moon's sudden disappearance, Madam Xiang

Rolling into a dark mass of clouds. How can you blame me
Half decomposed, half wistful and desperate for more?

No matter who it's given to, you and you and her,
Thinking of it or not—is it living?

He must be singing, the river wind caresses a
Scent of wild fruit and flowers between his legs

Under the river light. Finally, it's love. A beauty. One person exits
Or collectively dies for the integrity. It's love.

Mute song in the heart. An exit from the garden
Sagging with grapes, because of it. A raging fire.

A nice day, late summer evening
Watching the world as its misery approaches

A last intact stone
Stands still, as the high moon

Casts an illuminated self. Pick up a lotus, smile
At the distinguished face, fine coat, top hat, iridescent pearl . . .

Heaven sent flowers fall like rain, like rain.

7

他过世的时候，我在远方
不能再远。

这是我从来避免的话题。亲人
生动地死去，伴随烟，骨植碎裂，灰烬。

呼吸缓慢变浅，海潮
一浪，连额上的皱褶也湿润起来

一浪冲净落满尘土的记忆
你说，对不起……

以为不过一次短暂的告别
起锚，升帆，一粒盐就这样溶入海

从而无所不在。像夜的梦
刷地一下划亮充满寓意的歌 ——

远方，我脱下裙子，换上
爬山靴，准备再次上路。

记住你的血脉，读你遗赠的书
却不能走近你，对不起。

山倒了，地裂，光荣啊，
他的神，在供桌上合目不看。

7

At the moment he died, I was far I
Couldn't be farther.

It's the topic I try to avoid. Someone dear
Dies. Vividly, with smoke, broken bones, ashes.

Breath slows and becomes shallow, a tide, a wave
Stretches, turns the wrinkles on his forehead moist

And washes clean the dusty memory
You, saying, I'm sorry . . .

Thinking only of a brief separation
Sail set, cast away, a salt crystal dissolved by the sea

Then is everywhere. As last night's dream
Lights this song with meaning:

Far, I change, from skirt into
Hiking boots, preparing for another journey.

Thinking of you, my blood, reading the book you gave me
Yet unable to get close to you. I'm sorry.

The mountains fall! The earth cracks! Ah, glory
The god on his altar sees nothing.

8

最好我还是不认识你
从而想象你对我一往情深：

呵护我，现在用大毛巾
把这注活水一下子抱起来。

吸干，吮干，你会让我伤心。去吧
找一付桨和另外一条船

去很远的地方。九十九岁
瞎了眼，因为你已经知道太多。

比如男女的秘密
或者说神的秘密，将来。

于是，送给我这本古诗？
我的未来，你和我读不出的未来

漆黑。已经伸手不见五指了。
天亮的时候，你会追上你

游泳，顺流，在同一种色调上
你的水再次把你包裹

笑容，你和你消融。高潮时
一浪掀过眉头，铺展身底下的沙。

8

I've never met you, so
Imagine you lost in love.

Adore me like now, embrace me with a big towel—
This pool of spring water. Absolutely, in your arms.

Drink, kiss me dry, before you break my heart. Go then, sail your
Next boat, ride a new set of peddles

To a far away place. Ninety-nine
And blinded by knowing too much.

For example, this secret of man and woman,
The secrets of gods, the future.

Is it why you sent the ancient collection?
Poetry, my future, the blurred future of you and me

Pitch black. You already can't see the hand in front of your face.
At daybreak, you catch up with you

Swim downstream, the same color
Your water wraps you up

In laughter, the two of you merge. High tide climaxes
A wave over the eyebrows, the sand flattened underneath.

9

怎么形容海？
向一个从没见过海的人？

活了九十九岁，他想看海，想
走在玻璃海上并且吹响七只号角。

在这欢乐的一瞬间，大天使的翅膀
写出满天预言，我又怎么能

告诉他风暴，和呛人的海涛
海上发生的事情，我们之间是是非非？

海晒出盐，泪流成海
他看不见的预言是泪，世界。

在想象的岸上，他总比我们走得快
逝去的影子像披散的床单雪白

舔净汗津津的额角，无法形容的咸
把握这场旷日的健身运动。

溯游直上，腰承受水的重量
千年沉积。抓不住的爱。

他顺流，并不不追求什么。
他先我们进入大海。

9

How to describe sea
To someone who's never seen it?

He lives to ninety-nine, he wants it, to see it
To walk on its glass surface, to blow the seven trumpets.

At this joyous moment gigantic angel wings
Write prophesy all over the sky. How can I tell him

About sea storms, the choking waves
These things, right and wrong, that happen between us?

The prophesy he can't read is the world, tears
That become sea, sea that dries to salt.

On the brink of imagination, he's walking
Faster than us, a shadow white as our rumpled sheets.

Lick clean the moist forehead, the indescribable saltiness of the body
Building exercises that take the whole afternoon.

Resist the current, the waist laden with water sustains
A thousand years of sediment. The love that can't be contained.

He drifts downstream, pursues
Nothing. He enters the sea before us.

10

进入地底。

这间屋子。
没有风，也没有光。

因为你已经走了很远
或者住得太久。

我们在底层。不能感觉
这里思想彷徨。你的脚步

咚咚敲响我们头顶上
另外一个世界的晨钟。

你说，那里芙蓉遍地，永远湿润
我想象你舒服地呻吟，自由

在露天的花园拥抱。这就是
他把握的秘密？

睡下去吧，梦里的阳光忽明忽暗
还有白鹭和啄木鸟，风。

更深的地方。智慧以黄土的
形式为你们旋出恰当的洞穴

结实，而且适用，不会在作爱时
吱吱作响

没有光的深处一股泉－井？
井。这秘密小心将你们埋起。

10

Enter the underworld.

This room.
No wind, nor light.

Because you've already walked very far or
Stayed too long.

We are at the bottom. And can't sense
The thought walking back and forth. Your steps

Dong-Dong, striking above our head
The morning bell of another world

You say, there are lotus everywhere, always moist
You moan in my imagination, comfortable and free

To embrace in the open garden.
Is that the secret he holds?

Sleep away, sunlight in the dream flashes on and off
There will be white egrets and woodpeckers. Wind

Further down. Wisdom in the form of soil
Digs you a cave fitting

And sturdy, suitable, not squeaky
When you make love

At this lightless depth, a spring—a well?
A well: the secret meticulously buries you.

II

樱桃熟了。夏的结尾。
其中两颗落在我脚下花砖

皮开肉绽，甜香的结尾。树荫
竟容许如此惨烈的事情安静地发生。

挂在枝头并不诱人，毁灭之时
却格外艳丽：闪耀春天的光和色彩。

但愿只有春花和夏叶。
但愿你是上帝。

叹惜把她们拾起来，再次利用
榨汁或煮酱，献上灵台。

我是见证人。坐着，看见她们最后
唯一的飞行，为了看不见的籽。

或者只为飞，离开生了根的树
哪怕一瞬间。飞下崖。

把花砖移开，铺黄土，看她们
轻轻落入柔软的终床。

击水三千里。启锚，扬帆
他海一样的手掌。

II

Cherries ripe. The end of summer.
Two fall upon the flowered tiles under my feet

Bruised and lacerated, their sweet, fragrant end. The shadow of leaves
Allowing these brutal things to occur quietly.

While on the branches not so attractive, in their destruction turn
Splendid: shining with the light and color of spring.

Wish there were only spring flowers and summer leaves.
Wish you were a god.

Sigh, pick them up, reuse them
Squeezing juice or boiling jam, to put on your altar.

I am the witness. Sitting, watching their last
And only flight, the seeds invisible.

Or only for the flight, leaving the rooted tree
Even for just a moment. Leap from the cliff.

Remove the tiles, spread the soil, watch them
Gently, gently landing in their soft death bed.

Breaking the three thousand mile wave. Cast off, set sail
His sea hand.

12

教堂的门打开了。
牧师们站在向上的台阶微笑。

这杯清水，为远行的人解渴
归途匆匆。您的灵魂可以在这里解脱。

点燃的蜡烛浮在水上，浮出流动的河
欢迎，欢迎，今天是我的生日。

也是我写作的日子。好日子
无法进入教堂。因为你拉过我的手

以后发生了很多事情：
在如此明媚的阳光下采莲

还有樱桃坠地，滴血的葡萄
还有这片我们不认识的疆土，上面

新新旧旧的墓碑。先是她去了
后来他去了，她们去了，你。

准备着，我们一天又一天晨练
准备自己的心身，因为我们

肯定会获得这最终的秘密。请为我引路——
这些亡魂点亮的生日蜡烛

顺流船
能让我在海边追上？

12

Church doors open.
Priests standing up on the steps, smiling.

This cup of clean water to quench the thirst of travelers
On a hurried journey home. Where their souls may be free.

Lit candles float on water, become a river.
Welcome, welcome, today is my birthday.

My writing day as well. A good day though
I cannot enter the church—since you held my hand.

Lots of things have happened:
Picking lotus under this warm and tempting sun

And falling cherries, grapes dripping blood-like,
The unrecognizable land littered by

Tomb stones, old and new. First she is gone
Then he, they, you.

Preparing, we do morning exercise day after day
Prepare our body and soul,

Undoubtedly we'll receive the last secret. Please guide me—
These birthday candles lit by the dead souls

Downstream boats
Can I catch up with you at the edge of the sea?

13

一封退回的信。
有地址，还有照片，服饰整齐

连头发都梳得一丝不苟
那里曾经是一个灿烂的世界——

我们希望，我们年轻。
现在简装，企图把这个世界赋予的东西

统统交还。包括每一个早晨和月亮。
这是不是件好事？你问。

那么这些梦：手把着手
在沙滩上写出一行行白鸥

出海，去追他的帆。河入海
佩戴泡沫终极的莲冠

甜腥，还有几颗赤裸的卵石
从史前的雪山滚入平铺的手掌。

拈花一笑。他逝去的床
此刻竟温暖幽暗从而令人神往：

才意识到我们其实离海还远，离他
更隔了无法投递的思念。

海蓝的梦：天幕上海豚忘我地追逐。

13

A returned letter.
There is an address, and photographs of tidy clothes

Even the hair combed meticulously
Once there was a splendid world—

We hoped, we were young. Now we
Simplify, returning what this world has presented us

Everything. Including each morning and each moon.
Isn't it a good thing? You ask.

How about these dreams. Hand holding hand
On a sandy beach writes white gulls as line after line

Out to sea, chasing his sail. The river runs to sea
Wearing an ultimate lotus crown of foam

Sweet and fish-flavored, a few naked pebbles roll down from
Pre-historical snowcaps into the spread palm.

Pick up a lotus and smile. His death bed
Warm and quietly dark, very attractive for the moment:

Then we realize we are actually far from the sea, from him
Separated further by the undeliverable desire.

A sea blue dream: dolphins, with abandon, chase each other in the sky.

14

猛虎在城市大街上袭击
扑倒两个美女和一个孩子。

行人的脚步停下来，又再次纷纷走动
怎么会有这样的事发生？

还是夏天。荷花正盛。
生活刚刚开始，青春期梦游的光

不小心点亮这么些欢乐的蜡烛
都是瞬间的事，都为我目睹

翻腾出封闭在我们集体记忆里的
最后秘密：涉江，采芙蓉。

医生说不要喝酒或者吸烟。所以
我在健康表上老实填下

不喝酒，不吸烟。
不要吓唬孩子。不摘葡萄。

正是上班高峰。街边
纵欲的店铺还没摇起铁栅。

阳光，阳光，阳光 ——

都说，雨不会下来。

14

A tiger pounces on a city street
Striking down two beauties and a child.

Passersby stop, and then walk again in a continuous stream
How can such a thing happen?

It is still summer. Lotus blossoms.
Life has just begun, the light of a dream-walker in puberty

Carelessly burning abundant joyful candles
In a split moment, I see it all

Stirring up in our collective memory
The sealed secret: cross the river, pick the lotus.

The doctor says, do not drink or smoke.
I dutifully fill in the form,

Don't drink or smoke.
Don't threaten the child; don't pick grapes.

At the peak of rush hour. On the side of the street
Shops that satisfy carnal desires yet to raise their iron gates.

Sunlight, sunlight, sunlight—

They say no rain will come.

(*translated by Rachel Levitsky*)

Zhang Er was born in Beijing, China and moved to the United States in 1986. Her writings of poetry, non-fiction, and essays have appeared in publications in Taiwan, China, the American émigré community and in a number of American journals. She is the author of multiple books in Chinese and in English translation. She co-edited *First Line* and *Poetry Current*, Chinese poetry journals based in New York, and has participated in projects sponsored by the New York Council for the Arts (a Translation Award) and by the Minetta Brook Foundation (a Film Grant). She currently resides in Olympia, Washington.

Rachel Levitsky teaches English to immigrant members of DC9, New York City's painters union. She is the author of four chapbooks of poetry, *Dearly*, (a+bend), *Cartographies of Error* (Leroy), *The Adventures of Yaya and Grace* (Potes-Poets) and *2(1x1)Portraits* (Baksun). She organizes BELLADONNA*, a matrix (poetic readings, salons, chaplet press) of feminist poetics. Her long poem, *Under the Sun*, was published by Futurepoem in 2003.

Timothy Liu is the author of five books of poems, most recently *Of Thee I Sing* (University of Georgia) His first book of poems, *Vox Angelica* (Alice James Books), received the Norma Farber First Book Award from the Poetry Society of America. His other books of poems are *Burnt Offerings* (Copper Canyon Press), *Say Goodnight* (Copper Canyon Press), and *Hard Evidence* (Talisman House). An Associate Professor of English at William Paterson University, Liu lives in Hoboken, NJ.

Leonard Schwartz is the author of several collections of poetry, including *The Tower of Diverse Shores* (Talisman House), *Words Before The Articulate: New and Selected Poems*, (Talisman House), *Objects of Thought, Attempts At Speech* (Gnosis Press), and *Exiles:Ends* (Red Dust Press). He is also the author of a collection of essays *A Flicker At The Edge Of Things: Essays on Poetics 1987-1997* (Spuyten Duyvil) and co-editor of two anthologies of contemporary American poetry: *Primary Trouble: An Anthology of Contemporary American Poetry* and *An Anthology of New(American) Poets*.

Eleni Sikelianos's most recent books of poems are *The Monster Lives of Boys & Girls* (Green Integer, National Poetry Series) and *Earliest Worlds* (Coffee House Press). Forthcoming are *The California Poem* (Coffee House), and *The Book of Jon* (Nonfiction; City Lights). She teaches in the Writing & Poetics program at Naropa University, and in the Creative Ph.D. program at the University of Denver.

THE BOY WHO CATCHES WASPS
Selected Poems by Duo Duo
Translated by Gregory B. Lee

Duo Duo's poetic vision embraces a historical and political vision that is much more diverse, more global than that circumscribed by the confines of the last third of China's twentieth century. The context of China, Duo Duo's lived experience, is necessarily present, but it is diffused in a world-view that embraces all of modern humanity's dilemmas, our increasing separation from nature, and our alienation from one another.

"Duo Duo is one of the mountains in the topographical map of contemporary world poetry, and it's nearly scandalous that this excellent selection and translation by his long-time collaborator, Gregory Lee, is his first American book." —ELIOT WEINBERGER

$14.95 / 0-939010-70-4 / 216 PP

FUSION KITSCH
Poems by Hsia Yü
Translated by Steve Bradbury

While Hsia Yü may well have been one of the first woman poets writing in Chinese to have written about love and romance in a manner that broke dramatically from the conventions and constraints of traditional Chinese women's poetry, if we bother to look beyond labels at the poetry itself, we will find a body of work that is far less interested in providing a critique of gender relations or advancing a sexual/textual agenda than in exploring the sensuous and quirky interface between the pleasures of the flesh and the pleasures of the text.

"Hsia Yü explodes the stereotype of the reticent and passive Asian woman in one fell swoop. These poems seem to want to devour the world as they record it." —FRED MORAMARCO, POETRY INTERNATIONAL

$13.00 / 0-939010-64-X / 132 PP

FISSURES: CHINESE WRITING TODAY
Edited by Henry Zhao, Yanbing Chen, and John Rosenwald

An anthology of contemporary Chinese poetry, prose, and essays taken from the literary journal *Jintian* (*Today*). *Jintian* has been the foremost voice of contemporary Chinese writing since its inception on "The Democracy Wall" in Beijing in 1978, and its subsequent reinvention in 1989. This is the third volume in the series and the first undertaken by a U.S. publisher. Authors include Bei Dao, Gao Ertai, Yang Lian, and Zhu Wen—names that only continue to grow in importance as Chinese literature expands the Western canon.

"This anthology is a window into the minds & lives of some of the world's finest young writers."
—GARY SNYDER

$14.95 / 0-939010-59-3 / 108 PP